LIVEWIRE
REAL LIVES

Please return
on or before
date

CHELSEA

Mike Wilson

Published in association with The Basic Skills Agency

Hodder Murray

A MEMBER OF THE HODDER HEADLINE GROUP

The Publishers would like to thank the following for permission to reproduce copyright material:

Photo credits
p.2 © Rex Features/Action Press; p.6 © Popperfoto; p.10 © Action Images; p.14 © Action-Plus Photographic; p.16 © Heino Kalis/Reuters; p.20 © Olly Greenwood/Rex Features; p.23 © Ben Radford/Getty Images.

Orders: please contact Bookpoint Ltd, 130 Milton Park, Abingdon, Oxon OX14 4SB. Telephone: (44) 01235 827720. Fax: (44) 01235 400454. Lines are open from 9.00–6.00, Monday to Saturday, with a 24-hour message answering service. Visit our website at www.hoddereducation.co.uk.

© Mike Wilson 1998, 2005
First published in 1998 by
Hodder Murray, a member of the Hodder Headline Group
338 Euston Road
London NW1 3BH

Impression number   10 9 8 7 6 5 4 3 2 1
Year   2010 2009 2008 2007 2006 2005

Cover photo © Action Images/Alex Morton
Typeset in 14pt Palatino by SX Composing DTP, Rayleigh, Essex.
Printed in Great Britain by CPI Bath.

A catalogue record for this title is available from the British Library

ISBN-10 0 340 90078 4
ISBN-13 978 0 340 90078 9

Contents

In 2003, there was a revolution
at Chelsea Football Club.
It was a Russian revolution.

Chelsea FC had a new owner.
He was Roman Abramovich,
a millionaire from Russia.
He was the richest man in the UK.

Roman Abramovich had one simple plan.
He wanted Chelsea to win
in the UK and in Europe.
And he didn't care how much money it cost.

In 2003, the club was 98 years old.
Would Chelsea have more silverware to show off
in time for its 100-year-old birthday party?

Roman Abramovich, the richest man in the UK.

1 History

Before there was a Chelsea Football Club,
there was a sports ground at Stamford Bridge.
It was for athletics.

In 1905, some football players got together
at Stamford Bridge and made a team.
They called it Chelsea Football Club.

This was quite a late start.
Other London clubs,
like Spurs and Arsenal,
had been around for years.

At first, Chelsea were often in the shadow
of Spurs and Arsenal.

Even so, in their very first season,
Chelsea scored 90 goals in just 38 games.
The league has changed a lot since then.
But that's still the club record.

Right from the start,
Chelsea had an image.

Chelsea is a rich part of London.
The King's Road in Chelsea has always
been famous for style and fashion.

The football club was famous
for style and fashion too:
Chelsea FC had money.
They had class, and classy players.

But they never won anything.
Not until 50 years later – in 1955!
Then they won the League
for the first and only time!

They did come close in 1915.
That was in the FA Cup Final.
But Chelsea lost to Sheffield United.

2 Stars and Legends

The Hall of Fame at Chelsea
is full of the world's greatest players.

Jimmy Greaves played for Chelsea (1957–61).
Later, he was one of the first English players
to sign for a club in Italy.
He scored 132 goals in 169 games for Chelsea.
In his last season at Stamford Bridge,
Jimmy Greaves scored 41 goals in the League.
That's still the club record.

Chelsea's first world-class side
came together in the 1970s.

That team won the FA Cup in 1970.
The following year they won
the European Cup Winners' Cup.

Ron Harris lifts the FA Cup in 1970. Next to him, holding the Cup stand is Peter Bonetti.

In that side, every player was a character.
Every player was a star.
There was the goal keeper Peter Bonetti
known as 'The Cat'.

There was Ron Harris,
known as 'Chopper'.
He was the hard man of the defence.
'If he was in a good mood,' someone said,
'he'd put disinfectant on his studs
before he tackled you!'

Up front was Peter Osgood.
He played for Chelsea for 11 years:
1964–74 and again 1978–9.
He scored 150 goals.
'He has never been replaced,'
said one fan,
'since the day they let him go!'

It took years to build another team
as good as the Chelsea of the early 1970s.
Why did it take so long?

Winning came very easily to those players.
They were so good,
they didn't seem to have to work all that hard.
They began to think they didn't have to try at all!

When the dream team fell apart,
Chelsea lost their way.
At the end of the 1975–6 season,
they were eleventh in League Division Two.

It took 20 years to get back on top.

3 The Man Who Bought Chelsea FC for £1

In 1982, Chelsea was in trouble.
The club was struggling in Division Two,
and was £2 million in debt.

One man paid just £1 for Chelsea FC.
He was the Chairman, Ken Bates.

Matthew Harding also loved
Chelsea Football Club. He was the Vice-Chairman.
He helped to rebuild the team.
He had dreams of winning the Premiership.
Then his team would go on into Europe,
and win the European Championship.

But Matthew Harding didn't live long enough
to see his dreams come true.
He died in a helicopter crash in October 1996.

Everyone in football went into mourning,
and even Tony Blair went to Matthew's funeral.

Ken Bates (left) and Matthew Harding (right).

4 Chelsea International

The famous Chelsea side of the 1970s
was all British:
one or two Scots, the rest English.
In the 1990s,
the team became Chelsea International!

As well as home-grown talent,
there were players from Russia,
Norway, Romania, France and Italy.

It was easy for Chelsea
to attract world-class stars.
Chelsea was famous for style and class.
Then there was the £20,000 a week
Chelsea paid its top players.
(A lot of money, back then.)

And some joined Chelsea,
just because of the new manager,
Ruud Gullit.

Ruud Gullit was born in Holland.
He'd been European Player of the Year in 1987.
In 1989, he'd won the European Cup,
with AC Milan.
He came to Chelsea as a player in 1995.
A year later he took over as manager.

Ruud spent millions on new players.

The first big name player he signed
was Gianluca Vialli.
Vialli came from top Italian club Juventus,
on a free transfer in May 1996.
When Vialli took over as manager in February 1998,
he won five trophies in three years.
No other Chelsea manager
had had that kind of success.

Gianfranco Zola was a genius – and very popular.
He was Player of the Year in 1997 and 1999.
He scored 80 goals in over 300 games (1996–2003)
and helped to make hundreds more
for his grateful team mates.

Ruud Gullit took his team to Wembley
for the 1997 FA Cup Final.

Ruud was the first foreign manager
– and the first black manager –
to take a team to the FA Cup Final.
He was also the first to win.
Chelsea beat Middlesbrough 2–0.

Roberto di Matteo scored
after only 43 seconds!
This was the quickest goal ever
at a Wembley final!

It was Chelsea's first big win for 26 years.

For Ruud Gullit, this was just the beginning.
But Chairman Ken Bates had other ideas.
He sacked his manager in February 1998.

Gianluca Vialli – so many times
the man Ruud Gullit had left on the bench –
took over as manager.

Ruud Gullit with the team that won the 1997 FA Cup.
Sitting down with the Cup are:
Roberto di Matteo, Gianfranco Zola and Dennis Wise.
Kneeling down, on the right, is the man who took over
the job of Chelsea manager, Gianluca Vialli.

That same season, Chelsea went on
to win the European Cup Winners' Cup,
and the Coca-Cola Cup.

And they finished fifth in the Premiership.

Chelsea won the FA Cup again in 2000.
They beat Aston Villa 1–0.
And they beat Manchester United
in the FA Charity Shield.

It wasn't enough to keep Vialli in his job.
Four months later, he was sacked.
Another Italian, Claudio Ranieri,
stepped in to take his place.

Claudio Ranieri.

5 Second Best

Claudio Ranieri lasted four years.

In that time, Chelsea came close,
but they were always second best.

In 2002, they came sixth in the Premiership
for the second year running.
They also got to the FA Cup Final.
They lost 2–0 to Arsenal.

In 2003, Arsenal knocked them out again
– this time in the quarter-finals.
At the end of the season,
Chelsea finished fourth in the Premiership table.

For everyone at Chelsea,
coming close was not good enough.

In June 2003, Chairman Ken Bates
sold his share of Chelsea Football Club
to Roman Abramovich for £17 million.

Suddenly, there was plenty more money
to invest in new players.
Ranieri spent over £100 million:
on Damien Duff, Wayne Bridge;
on Mutu, Crespo and Makelele.

But Chelsea still crashed out
in the semi-finals of the Champions' League.
And they came second – to Arsenal –
in the Premiership in 2004.

Chelsea had to look to the future.

Ken Bates finally stepped down as Chairman
in March 2004.
Two months later,
Claudio Ranieri also left Chelsea.

He was replaced by José Mourinho.
Mourinho's club, Porto, from Portugal,
had just won the Champions' League.

6 Hungry for Success

In his first year at Chelsea,
Roman Abramovich spent over £240 million.
Some of it was paying off the club's debts.
But most of it was on new footballers.

New manager José Mourinho
bought two key players
from his old club Porto:
Paulo Ferreira and Ricardo Carvalho.
He also bought Didier Drogba
from French side Marseille.

The new players had a lot in common:
they were all world-class players.

And they were all hungry for success.

Didier Drogba scores against Porto in the Champions' League in 2004.

Mourinho knows
that big-money players
don't make a world-class team.

You also need to work hard, train hard,
think as a team and be a tight squad.
'You have to think,' he says,
'for every second of every match.'

And you might need a little luck.

In September 2004,
Chelsea played in the Champions' League.
They played the Champions, FC Porto –
José Mourinho's old side – and beat them 3–1.

Chelsea are still building their new team.

But they are looking very strong.

The year 2005 would be a good year
for Chelsea football club to win a major trophy.
Chelsea will be 100 years old.
As yet, there is not enough to show
for 100 years of football.
Not enough Cup wins, not enough League wins.
Not enough success in Europe…

Not enough glory
has come home to Stamford Bridge.

But now, there is the tactical genius
of José Mourinho.
And there is the money of Roman Abramovich.
This is the best chance they'll ever have.

It's now or never for Chelsea Football Club.

José Mourinho.

7 Chelsea – Timeline

1905 Chelsea Football Club founded
at Stamford Bridge

1907 Went up to League Division One

1915 Runners-up in the FA Cup Final

1935 Record attendance at Stamford Bridge:
82,905 (against Arsenal)

1953 Worst defeat ever: 8–1 against Wolves

1955 Won League Division One

Won the FA Charity Shield

1965 Won the League Cup

1967 Runners-up in the FA Cup Final

1970 Won the FA Cup for the first time

1971 Biggest win ever:
13–0 in European Cup Winners' Cup

Won the European Cup Winners' Cup

1983 Ended the season
eighteenth in Division Two

1984 Won League Division Two

1988 Ended the season
eighteenth in Division Two

1989 Won League Division Two

1994 Runners-up in the FA Cup Final

1997 Won the FA Cup for the second time

1998 Won the League Cup

Won the European Cup Winners' Cup

Won the European Super Cup

2000 Won the FA Cup for the third time

Won the FA Charity Shield

2002 Runners-up in the FA Cup Final

2004 Runners-up in the Premiership

8 Chelsea – Quiz

How much can you remember about Chelsea?
Can you quickly look back through the book
to find the answers?

1   In what year was Chelsea Football Club
     founded?

2   In what year did Chelsea win the League
     for the first time?

3   How many goals did Jimmy Greaves
     score for Chelsea?

4   What did Chelsea win in 1970?

5   Where was Ruud Gullit born?

6   How long did it take Roberto di Matteo
     to score for Chelsea in the 1997
     FA Cup Final?

7   How many trophies did Chelsea win
    under manager Gianluca Vialli
    from 1998 to 2000?

8   What country is Roman Abramovich from?

9   How much money did he spend
    in his first year at Chelsea?

10 What country is José Mourinho from?

11 What club did he manage
    before he came to Chelsea?

12 In 2005, how old was Chelsea Football Club?